Pubs of Wimbledon Village
(Past & Present)

By
Clive Whichelow

Published by

Enigma Publishing
4 Charnwood Avenue
London SW19 3EJ

First edition October 1998

ISBN 0 9524297 13

By the same author:
Mysterious Wimbledon (with Ruth Murphy) ISBN 0 9524297 0 5
More Mysterious Wimbledon (with Ruth Murphy) ISBN 0 9524297 5 6

Printed by Roebuck Press

CONTENTS

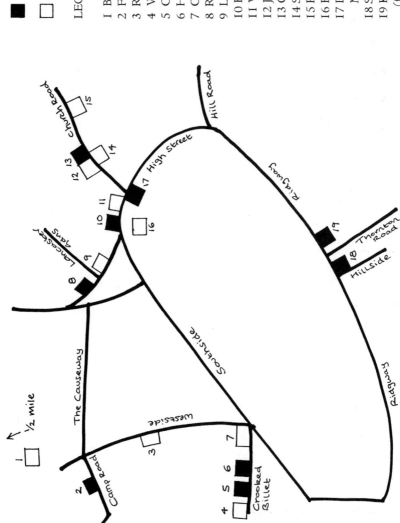

LEGEND

■ Present pub

□ Past pub

1 Baldfaced Stag
2 Fox & Grapes (formerly Union)
3 Rising Sun
4 Wheatsheaf Brewery
5 Crooked Billet (present building)
6 Hand in Hand
7 Crooked Billet (18th century)
8 Rose & Crown
9 Lord Palmerston
10 Brewery Tap
11 Wimbledon Brewery
12 Jolly Butchers
13 Castle
14 Swan (formerly White Hart)
15 Red Lyon
16 Beehive
17 Dog & Fox (formerly Sign of
   My Lord's Arms)
18 Swan
19 King of Denmark
   (formerly Jolly Gardeners)

PUBS OF WIMBLEDON VILLAGE (PAST AND PRESENT)

INTRODUCTION

'There is nothing which has yet been contrived by man, by which so much happiness is produced as by a good tavern or inn.'
Dr. Samuel Johnson 21st of March 1776

A short walk around Wimbledon Village will tell you that there are nine pubs, but hidden in the mists of time are a further dozen inns, taverns, and alehouses of Wimbledon past.

Some have been replaced by later pubs, some have merged with existing ones, one still lives on as a private house, and some are remembered in name only. And what names! The Cock & Hoope, The Beehive, The Jolly Butchers...

From the time of Henry VIII through the days of stagecoaches, prize-fights, and Victorian poets to the present, these inns and taverns have seen the growth of Wimbledon from a small clutch of cottages to the sprawling town of today.

But some of the magic lingers on, and in the best of the Wimbledon Village pubs one can still enjoy a good pint of beer and conversation much as the poet John Taylor did in the 1600s. And if you look carefully you can still see glimpses of past glories: low ceilings, oak beams, adjoining stables, and Georgian splendour nestling behind modern facades.

Along with the church, the village pub was often the centre of the community both figuratively and literally, and many early village meetings were held there. Decisions that affected the growth and prosperity of Wimbledon were made in pubs such as the Rose & Crown and Dog & Fox when vestry meetings adjourned from St. Mary's Church. The pub acted as village hall, town council chamber and courtroom, as well as a centre for fun, frivolity and relaxation. It also served as a games room, newsagents, betting shop and sports centre – the forerunners of Wimbledon FC even used the Fox & Grapes and the Swan as their changing rooms!

Perhaps more than any other institution the pub reflects the monumental changes of the past five hundred years, and through its history reveals much about who we are, not to mention who we were.

So, pour yourself a drink and sit back and enjoy a tour round the Wimbledon Village pubs – past and present.

A BRIEF HISTORY OF PUBS

When you have lost your inns drown your empty selves, for you will have lost the last of England - Hillaire Belloc

To see the rise of the Wimbledon Village pubs in perspective it is essential to know something of the background against which they developed. There have been pubs in Wimbledon since at least the time of Henry VIII. The tavern which stood on the site of what is now the Dog & Fox was run by a Margery Haynes in those days, and later, in the reign of James I by Mary Walker.

It was not unusual for a tavern to be run by a woman, as it was women who had been the original 'brewsters' in the early alehouses. These were the first public houses – ordinary dwelling houses open to the public for the consumption of ale made on the premises. But over the centuries these alehouses became inns and taverns and were mainly shaped by four things: travel, The Church, war, and the law.

Before the building of the Roman roads, travel was arduous and to be avoided unless absolutely necessary, so there was little need for places of refreshment along the way. However, once the roads were in place and people began to travel further afield taverns and inns began to appear.

Taverns usually served wine and food, but providing no accommodation, were not intended for the long distance traveller. He was catered for by the inn, which principally provided food and lodging, plus wine and ale if required.

After the Roman occupation the number of such establishments increased, and as early as the 10th century King Edgar decreed that there were too many alehouses and that they should be restricted to one in each village. By this time the distinctions between inns, taverns, and alehouses had already begun to blur and it is likely that all three provided some sort of food, lodging, and even entertainment.

In 1215 the Magna Carta declared that there should be 'standard measures for wine, ale and corn', and although the standard measure for beer continues to this day, it is interesting to note that there is no such thing for a serving of wine in a modern pub.

It now seems odd to think that the church helped build the institution of the public house, but this is exactly what happened when medieval churches and monasteries provided hospices, or hostels, for pilgrims and other travellers. These offered food and lodging, and their ale was said to be the best in the land! Of course, at the time, ale was the principal drink for all members of the family. Tea and coffee had yet to be introduced, and clean water was not always readily available. So the church could not be accused of leading people to the evils of drink. Although in medieval times there were 'Church Ales' when villagers would contribute barley to be brewed by the church and sold back to them as ale during religious festivals such as Easter and Christmas. And some of these were said to degenerate into drunken orgies.

In the 15th century hops were brought over from Holland, and British beer, more or less as we know it today, was born (ale had no hops). In the following century gin and sherry were introduced into Britain: gin from Holland (its name is derived from genever, the Dutch word for juniper from whose berries it is made), and sherry, or sack from Portugal.

The next big change in the development of pubs came with Henry VIII's dissolution of the monasteries in 1539, which, incidentally, was carried out by Thomas Cromwell who held the manor of Wimbledon at the time. The attached hospices fell into private hands and became inns. A further change came soon afterwards in 1552 when JPs were given the power to license and suppress alehouses, foreshadowing the licensing laws of today. In 1553 a further act limited to one the number of taverns allowed in each town, with some exceptions for larger cities (e.g. London was allowed forty), although by the turn of the century their number had risen again. Wimbledon, which was outside London in those days had two inns by 1617 – The Sign of My Lord's Arms (predecessor to the Dog & Fox), and The Sign of the White Hart in Church Road.

It wasn't until the Puritan era of the middle of the 17th century that publicans again felt under siege. Following the Civil War, and despite the fact that Oliver Cromwell's own mother was a brewster, the new regime banned Church Ales and Maypoles, taxed beer and ale for the first time, and made it illegal to buy or sell beer on a Sunday. Also, around the same period, tea, coffee and chocolate were introduced to this country – another threat to alehouse keepers. A third factor affecting them during this era was the rise of the breweries who were now supplying the publicans who had previously brewed their own beer.

The Restoration however was a welcome return to more convivial times, and this was clearly celebrated in Wimbledon when a relatively new inn known as the Sign of the Rose became The Rose and Crown.

By the turn of the 18th century the coaching era was underway, and inns became important stopping points for not only the travellers to obtain food and lodging but also for the essential change of horses. The standards went up to cater for this new trade, and at the same time alehouses began to improve their facilities to counteract the demand for cheap gin which was by now becoming something of a problem.

The next boost for the brewery trade was in 1780 when Lord North put a tax on malt to help finance the civil war in America. This tax, being as great for private individuals as for large concerns, effectively squeezed out the small brewers and by 1816 half the pubs in London were owned by, or tied to the breweries.

However, the most cataclysmic change to the industry came in 1830 when the Duke of Wellington introduced his Sale of Beer Act which was intended to encourage beer drinking in the face of the over-consumption of cheap spirits. This was effectively the Big Bang as far the pub business was concerned. Suddenly, anyone, regardless of character, who could pay two guineas for a licence could run a beer house. Within six years the number of beer houses had virtually doubled from 24,000 to 46,000. How ironic that the acronym for this act was SOBA!

Seven out of the nine existing Village pubs date from this act, not to mention a further two, The Lord Palmerston and The Beehive, which had come and gone by the end of the 19th century.

By 1869 something had to be done to curb the burgeoning beer shops, and the Wine and Beer House Act was introduced to limit their number. The result was that the breweries, realising that the outlets for their beer would be severely restricted, moved quickly to tie as many of the remaining ones to them as possible.

In 1872 a further attempt was made to limit the number of liquor licences, and also to restrict opening hours, however, the Intoxicating Liquors Bill was defeated - with the help of an unlikely supporter. The Archbishop of York said 'Better that England should be free than that England should be compulsorily sober'; and 'Better free than sober' became something of a catch-phrase for drinkers of the day.

While the attempts of various governments to harness the industry went on through the 19th century another revolution had been taking place. The railways had begun in the 1820s and by the middle of the century had, by and large, seen off the old stagecoaches. Although for every lost Coach and Horses, there may now have been a Whistle Stop, or Junction Tavern, an era was over, and some of the more remote inns struggled to keep going. Among them no doubt, the 17th century coaching inn known as the Baldfaced Stag at the edge of Wimbledon Common on the old Portsmouth Road.

With the new railway sufficiently distant none of this would have had a great deal of effect on the Wimbledon Village pubs however, but the next revolution which they had to withstand was the temperance movement.

Around the time of the Duke of Wellington's 1830 act a temperance movement had already got underway, with the London branch headed by Charles Blomfield, the Bishop of London. Then the Band of Hope formed in 1847, and by the turn of the century had two million members.

In Wimbledon, the first temperance meeting was held in the Village Club on the Ridgway in 1868. Canon Haygarth, the vicar of Wimbledon, declared 'In this parish the evils of drink are too apparent; it is the destroyer of domestic happiness, the bane of honest toil, the ruin of body and soul.' A decision was made to erect a drinking fountain, which still stands today, at the top of Wimbledon Hill. The promise of clean drinking water however was not enough to lure people from the pubs, and in the 1870s and 1880s several coffee taverns were opened. The Welcome, The Hope, The Wimbledon Coffee Palace, and others attracted a certain number of people, but still the pubs flourished. At least until the intervention of DORA.

The Defence Of the Realm Act, and a prior act were introduced soon after the start of the First World War in an attempt to reduce drunkenness among munitions factory workers. Lloyd George commented 'We are fighting Germany, Austria, and drink, and the greatest of these deadly foes is drink'.

Tax on drink was increased, its strength reduced, and pub opening hours were severely shortened. It even became an offence to buy someone else a drink. This Draconian strategy worked, and by the end of the war alcohol consumption had more than halved. The restricted opening hours remained for over seventy years and were only relaxed again by Mrs Thatcher's government in the late 1980s.

Perhaps the only counterbalance to all this as far as the publicans were concerned was the rise and rise of motor car use in the 20th century. This probably saved from closure some of the more remote pubs which had been hanging on since the latter days of the coaching era.

The next major change for Wimbledon's pubs came in 1965 when Wimbledon ceased to be in Surrey, and became part of Greater London. This meant that pubs could stay open until 11.00 p.m. on Sundays instead of having to call last orders at 10.30.

The 20th century continues to see further changes in pubs: from the domination of the big breweries to the Campaign for Real Ale, to the spread of multiples, or chains, to theme pubs, electronic games, giant TV screens, comedy clubs, pub theatre, live music, alcopops, and all-day opening. But despite all this, some of the Village pubs manage to retain a timeless charm, and it is reassuring to note that the Wimbledon Village pubs with the fewest gimmicks remain the most popular.

1881 ADVERTISEMENT

BREWERY TAP 1934 (BEFORE IT WAS EXTENDED)

BREWERY TAP

Although not a large pub today, the Brewery Tap in the High Street has been extended twice from its humble beginnings as a tap house/beer shop attached to the brewery* next door.

The first mention of a brewer and beer retailer on this site is in 1832 when William Cook was here. The name Brewery Tap does not appear until 1867 when the beer shop and brewery were being run by Robert Patterson. It was probably quite a small brewery, and a larger one was built in 1885 by William Quartermaine who had taken over the original premises in 1880. Whether or not Mr Quartermaine had a premonition we shall never know but he sold the brewery to Leonard McMullen in 1888 just months before it was destroyed by fire in January 1889.

Ironically, the burnt-out site was purchased later that year by the local council (for £1500.00) to build a fire station. The fire engines were kept here, but the horses were stabled behind the Dog & Fox – so it was doubtless a time-consuming task to get to a fire quickly.

In the early years of this century the Brewery Tap continued as a small beer shop, taking up just the small section on the southern side beneath the lower of the two existing roofs. It was bought in 1920 by Whitbread, who, in the 1930s, purchased the antiques shop next door and extended the pub, doubling its size. It now had two bars: saloon and public, and increased cellarage.

In 1954 the pub was taken over by Reg Lovett who ran it until the 1980s. It was still a cosy little pub with an open fire in the saloon bar, and the atmosphere of a private living room. In the increasingly competitive modern era that was unlikely to last, and it didn't.

In 1995 the pub was extended again, this time to the rear, and was now open-plan, the original two bars having been made one earlier that decade. So, despite the enlargements, the Brewery Tap remains Wimbledon Village's smallest pub, and although it has a jukebox, it still provides traditional pub games such as dominoes and backgammon – a game which dates back to the mid-17th century, almost two hundred years before this Village pub was built.

The present pub is not over-modernised and can proudly offer five different cask bitters – perhaps more choice than when there was a brewery next door!

* See section on breweries

CASTLE 1913 – NOTE ENTRANCE TO STABLES TO RIGHT

CASTLE

A lot about the history of a building can be learned by simply looking at the top half. Whilst the street level façades change almost by the decade, the original buildings above and behind reveal much about their history.

And so it is with the Castle in Church Road. The façade is one seamless pub exterior, but above, it is clear that there are two separate buildings. The one to the east, the original Castle pub, was built at the end of the Georgian era in the 1820s. The building to the west was formerly the Jolly Butchers – a Victorian beer shop which merged with the Castle at the beginning of this century (see separate entry for the Jolly Butchers).

The first mention of a beer shop on the Castle site was in 1845 when it was run by James Johnson. Before this it was almost certainly a private dwelling house, having been occupied by four consecutive tenants since 1828 when it was built. The original 80 year lease for 'newly-erected cottages and messuages' was priced at £12.6s.0d.

The pub was bought by brewers Thorne Brothers in 1900 when owner James Oakman died, and merged with the Jolly Butchers by 1903. Previously, the 'Butchers', with its appropriate sawdust on the floor, had served the working men as the trade-related name suggests, while the Castle had been frequented by a 'better class' of drinker. In fact, for a brief while in 1903 and 1904 the newly-merged pub was known as the Jolly Butchers, but by 1905 the name had reverted to the Castle.

In the 1890s it had had to endure even more competition when the Welcome Reading and Coffee Room opened up near the corner of the High Street (where the Rajdoot restaurant now stands). This had been set up by the temperance movement to entice people away from the evils of drink. The owners of the Castle were probably relieved when the Welcome later moved to larger premises further away in the High Street.

In the Victorian era many of the Village pubs ran livery stables, horse-drawn cab businesses, and carrier services, and the Castle was no exception. We know that in the 1860s the owner, Charles Yexley was listed in the trades directories as not only 'beer retailer', but also as 'carrier'. The stables were at the back of the pub, and remained there well into this century. By the 1930s they were being used by a riding school who leased the property from the Meux brewery who now owned it, and there were stalls for nine horses. The side alley entrance to the old stables is now used as an additional table area for the pub.

In modern times the Castle has had at least two claims to fame. The licensee in the 1960s and 70s was George Hardy, a former soccer professional with Queen's Park Rangers; and in the same period the pub was known to be actor Oliver Reed's local. There were even pictures on the wall to prove it!

The Castle had a major facelift in the 1980s and is now a very modern Allied Domecq pub with games machines, music, and large TV screens showing sport. However, the shell of the Georgian property remains to be seen for anyone who cares to simply look up.

CROOKED BILLET 1885

CROOKED BILLET

Q. How many historians does it take to change a light bulb?
A. Five. One to change the bulb, one to record when it was changed, and another three to argue about the date.

There is more disagreement over the origins of this pub than any other in the Village. Some put its beginnings as early as 1509, some say 1759, but what is indisputable is that the original Crooked Billet was not on the site of today's pub.

The first Crooked Billet was further down the road near the corner by the Common, and it is likely that it was there by 1745 when a vestry meeting was held at 'Thomas Wray's' who was the alehouse keeper of the Crooked Billet. Vestry meetings at this time were adjourned to pubs such as John Inward's (Dog & Fox), Richard Carter's (Rose & Crown), Joseph Townsend's (Rising Sun), and Widow Eade's (Swan – the original Swan in Church Road, not the later pub of the same name in the Ridgway).

Thomas Wray continued as alehouse keeper here until 1786 at which time he disappears from the list of Surrey victuallers. He died in 1794.

The 1509 start date for this pub does not seem to have any foundation in public records and can probably be discounted, as can the claim that this area was once 'Cromwell's half acre'. It seems that Walter Cromwell, father of Henry VIII's secretary Thomas, moved to Wimbledon in 1513, and died three years later, but there is no evidence to suggest that he either lived in the Crooked Billet area or ran an alehouse there.

The earliest mention of the Crooked Billet on its present site is in 1838 when run by William Williams who was there until 1881. The beginnings of the modern pub date back therefore to the 'big bang' of the Duke of Wellington's 1830 act. It is interesting to note that in the trade directories Williams was described between 1870 and 1881 as beer retailer and shopkeeper, though what he was selling apart from his beer we are not told. Although in the 1851 census he is mysteriously described as 'retailer of beer and coals'.

The Billet has sold Young's beer for over a century now, Young's having held the leasehold from 1888, and the freehold from 1928. The pub has been fashionable since the 1960s but regulars remember it being an old-fashioned local and can recall a bonfire being built on the green outside every November 5th as recently as the 1950s. In 1969 the pub was extended into the adjoining property – formerly the builder's merchants G. Dowden which had been there since the 1880s.

Although the pub has been modernised, most recently in 1994, it retains an 'olde worlde' atmosphere, and there are even tales of the ghost of an Irish woman who haunts the cellars. The pub also boasts a large barn-like restaurant at the back, and in summer accommodates many of its drinkers on the green at the front.

NOTE: The photograph of the Crooked Billet shown here was for many years thought to be of the Hand in Hand but it is in fact the original building which was probably replaced with the present building soon after the photo was taken.

DOG & FOX

An inn has stood on this site since at least the reign of Henry VIII when it was run by Margery Haynes, so the site at least can lay undisputed claim to being the oldest of any of the existing Village pubs.

No name is recorded for the inn until 1617 when it was known as the Sign of My Lord's Arms (see 'names' section). In a survey of the manor for Thomas Cecil, the Earl of Exeter, the inn is described as follows: 'An inne by Wimbledon pound, eight rooms, two butteries, two barns, a stable, and yard.' The pound, for stray animals, was just across the street where the old fire station now stands, and the 'butteries' were drink stores (thought to come from the French *bouteillerie*, or bottle store).

By 1776 when a map of Wimbledon was commissioned by the Lord of the Manor Earl Spencer, the inn was known as the Fox & Dog, and was being run by Edward Winchester who was there from 1748-1783. He was heavily involved in the running of the Village and at various times held the vestry offices of Surveyor of the Highways, Churchwarden, and Overseer - whose role it was to distribute funds from rates to the poor. The vestry meetings were often held here as well as at the Rose & Crown and other taverns and alehouses.

Later that century the Dog & Fox as it was by then known became the centre for excited activity when in 1797 there were rumours of an imminent invasion of Britain by Napoleon. A uniformed volunteer force of cavalry and foot soldiers was set up and they were given sword practice at the inn, and were trained on the Common. The threat passed however, and by 1802 the Wimbledon volunteers had disbanded.

More light-hearted activity was indulged in at the annual Easter fair, when the road from the Dog & Fox to the Rose & Crown was abuzz with 'booths, stalls, theatres, and menageries'. The Village fair was a popular event in the second half of the 18th century, and although exuberantly enjoyed by the working class villagers, was looked on with disdain by some of the gentlemen and ladies of the parish including Lord of the Manor Earl Spencer. He believed that it was 'London blackguards' from the Village fair who had broken into his wine cellar at the manor in 1785 and proceeded to get extremely drunk. It was however not until 1840 that the fair was suppressed by the local vicar and others for having a 'bad moral effect'.

Today of course, the annual Village fair is again part of the local social calendar but does not seem to be adversely affecting the morals of the local community.

By the time the Village fair had been ended there was at least a bowling green behind the Dog & Fox for the diversion of villagers. This game, which dates back to the 13th century, remained popular and was still being played there when the pub was rebuilt in 1869. By the next century most pub games were of the indoor variety and pictures of the Dog & Fox in the early part of this century show the 'billiard saloon' being prominently advertised.

Throughout the 1800s the Dog & Fox was the terminus for the London stagecoach. Starting around 1780, the coach, which went via Clapham to Gracechurch Street was by 1824 going twice a day, at 9.00 a.m. and 5.00 p.m. Aside from carrying passengers, it also carried mail, and brought the London newspapers to Wimbledon.

By 1902, after more rebuilding in 1900, the inn was known by the grander name of the Wimbledon Hill Hotel, and the earlier tradition of philanthropy continued as it hosted concerts for the Wimbledon Orphen's (sic) Society. A programme dated February 18th 1902 promised 'glassophone solos' by Mr Fred Burton, a 'sleight of hand performance' by Mr William Vincent, and 'a few imitations' by Mr Geo. Robins.

Today, the pub is again known as the Dog & Fox, and has an adjoining restaurant and function room, as well as stables (for a riding school) - not too far from where gentlemen tethered their horses almost five hundred years ago. Still owned by Young's, as it has been since 1834, the Dog & Fox remains a popular pub at the very heart of Wimbledon Village.

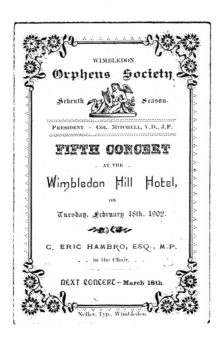

FOX & GRAPES 1908 (BEFORE IT WAS EXTENDED)

FOX & GRAPES

There is a local myth that this was once a 'tea and gin shop' and that it is over 300 years old, but there seems to be no support for either of these claims in local records. What we do know is that there has been a pub on this site in Camp Road since at least 1838. At that time it was known as the Union beer shop and was run by Charles Taylor (see separate entry). In the early 1800s, a local builder named William Croft had erected several cottages in West Place where he lived, as well as in Camp Road, and one of these cottages was probably the predecessor to the Fox & Grapes. Croft's son, Thomas, was a 'beer retailer' from 1832-34 although no pub name is mentioned in the records.

At that time even the road name was different - Workhouse Lane. The workhouse, which had been set up in 1752 by the local vestry was cleared of its inhabitants in 1834 under the Poor Law Amendment Act, but the name stuck for another thirty years. It was later known as Almshouse Lane when this type of dwelling replaced the workhouse, and later still as School Lane.

Until the 20th century the beer shop was much smaller than the present Fox & Grapes, occupying only what is now known as Caesar's Bar (named after nearby Caesar's Camp) – the small lower bar to the west. It is even believed that this small bar was further divided into two originally.

By 1868 the Union had become the Fox & Grapes, and twenty years after that was used as a changing room for what later became the cup-winning Wimbledon FC. The 'Dons' grew out of a team of old boys from the Old Central School in Camp Road. Formed in 1889, the Old Centrals' first pitch was on Wimbledon Common. The Fox & Grapes was a handy place to change, and no doubt provided refreshment after a hard match!

The team did have one piece of bad luck here though. In their debut game for the local Herald Cup in 1892 their dressing room was robbed of money and a watch and chain. To add insult to injury they lost the match too – four nil. It seems that the theft may have been a factor in their next choice of changing room; by the following season they were donning their new strip at the Swan in the Ridgway. (However, when the club won the FA cup in 1988 they returned to the Fox & Grapes afterwards for their celebrations).

By 1892, although still small, the pub was now fully licensed and had stabling for two horses and was owned by Atlee & Co. of Tooting (as was the King of Denmark in the Ridgway). There was also a 'carrier' by the name of James Booth next door who probably had stabling in addition to that of the Fox & Grapes.

The pub was enlarged in 1928 when it was extended into the eastern part of the building, which is believed to have previously been a laundry. Further rebuilding in the 1970s revealed an old well in the pub cellar.

This Inntrepreneur pub today remains largely traditional, and the original, lower bar especially, retains a country pub atmosphere. Long may it continue!

HAND IN HAND c.1930

HAND IN HAND

A quart of ale is a dish for a king
William Shakespeare

Although now a Young's pub the Hand in Hand stands on the site of a Watney's house. Not a Watney's pub that is, but the house of Daniel Watney who moved here in the 1730s, and whose great grandson founded the famous brewery. In fact, one of the early Watney family, William, had a small brewery in the Crooked Billet area in the 1770s (see Breweries section).

The present Hand in Hand started in 1865 as a bakery and grocers run by William Holland. By 1867 he was selling beer too, and two years later bought the property from Thomas Watney who had inherited it. The bakery continued and villagers would bring their Sunday dinners to be cooked in the bread ovens for a small fee of twopence.

The pub stayed in the Holland family for over a hundred years and did not even have a full licence until 1974 when it was bought by Young's brewery. The pub was much enlarged in a major refurbishment in 1981, and although sympathetically done, some of the rustic village atmosphere was inevitably lost. Locals remembered the tiny front bar with its carved antique chair, the wooden barrels of fruit wine and the country pub atmosphere.

When John Young came from the brewery to reopen the newly-refurbished pub in 1981 he was presented with a wreath by one of the regulars to 'commemorate the death of the pub he loved'. His name was Duncan Holland – a descendant of the founder perhaps? But Youngs must have done something right as the following year the 'Hand' won the Evening Standard Pub of the Year award – one of only two in Wimbledon Village to have done so (the other being the Rose & Crown).

Perhaps the interior of the pub was not the main focus of its customers' affections anyway; the little courtyard with its overhanging horse chestnut tree is unchanged, the green outside is as ever an attraction on summer evenings, and the Hand remains one of the best-loved of the Village's pubs.

The refurbishment also seems to have uncovered a ghost. In the mid 1980s a member of staff unlocked what she thought was an empty pub only to find a young girl with long dark hair and a white dress standing just beyond the corner of the original bar, but before she could be challenged she disappeared into thin air.

This year the Hand finally won CAMRA's South West London Pub Of The Year contest after being a finalist several times previously.

WIMBLEDON. — THE RIDGEWAY.

Best Wishes

KING OF DENMARK c.1910

KING OF DENMARK

The architect Samuel Teulon, who built not only the Village club in the Ridgway, but also Christ Church in Copse Hill, was commissioned to build cottages in the 1860s to ease the overcrowded housing of the poor. These cottages in the Ridgway were followed by shops and the King of Denmark pub, to serve the community which had been growing since the 1820s.

The earliest mention of the King is 1866 when it was being run by Thomas Roker, who was there for eleven years. The pub gave its name to both Denmark Terrace in which it stands, and also later to Denmark Road. There had been a small beer shop known as the Jolly Gardeners here since at least 1838 (see separate entry), but it was succeeded by the King.

By the turn of the century the King of Denmark was owned by the brewery company Messrs. Atlee & Co. of Tooting and although not a large pub it had stabling for five horses in the 1890s when run by Nathan Bond. This seems odd, as the larger Swan nearby, which ran regular coach services to Wimbledon Station, had stabling for only four horses. The answer may well be that the 'fly proprietor' A. Bailey, who was in Denmark Road in the 1880s could have used the stables at the King for his business.

The pub was rebuilt in the 1930s, and obtained a spirit licence in 1948. Regulars remember the odd layout of the pub when the present central door led down a narrow corridor to an off-sales counter at the bar. The Public and Saloon bars at either side were only accessible through their own separate doors, so if you wanted to go from one bar to the other it had to be via the street.

In the 1960s the pub was actually visited by its namesake, the King of Denmark! He was accompanied by his daughter Princess Marguerite, who in 1972 became the first Queen of Denmark for six hundred years. It is not known what prompted the royal visit but it was followed in the 1970s by a visit from another 'queen' - Miss Denmark.

The pub's image seems to have veered between the exotic and the homely over the years – at one time it housed a collection of Dickens' prints and African spears, while in the 1970s the landlord Jack Fuller was said to be partial to cooking sausages and potatoes over an open fire for customers.

The King is now a Sanderson pub, part of the Scottish & Newcastle group, and has just been refurbished (August 1998), although the alterations are hard to spot. Apart from the removal of a gantry round the bar, the interior has remained much the same and it remains a popular and friendly local.

The pub has retained a traditional feel with its wood panelling, darts, and lack of gimmicks although like most pubs it has been open-plan for some years. It has a small courtyard at the back, and benches at the front and remains a relaxing place from which to watch the world go by in the Ridgway.

ROSE & CROWN 1875

ROSE & CROWN

'When I find myself in the little room with the window open and the garden before us
and a glass of claret on the table, care seems to be excluded'
Poet Leigh Hunt writing of the Rose & Crown in the 1840s

This is Wimbledon's oldest inn still standing in its original form, and arguably the most important. Built c.1650 it later became the venue for vestry meetings adjourned from St. Mary's Church, and for meetings of the local friendly society.

It is known that the inn was here by 1659 as a trade token held at Wimbledon Museum bears this date as well as that of the then landlord T.E. Heburne. At that time, during the Commonwealth, the inn was known as the Sign of the Rose, the 'Crown' not being added until after the Restoration in 1660.

The only clue that this inn may have been in existence in some form earlier in the century was when Treswell's survey of the manor in 1617 showed a bowling alley at the site. These were usually adjacent to inns or taverns, though an inn was not specifically mentioned in the survey.

By the 18th century church vestry meetings were often being adjourned to local inns and taverns and although there are no records prior to 1735 we know that in 1745 they were being held at, amongst others, 'Richard Carter's' (i.e. the Rose & Crown). Originally formed to discuss matters relating directly to the church, the meetings began to take on a wider remit including upkeep of the highways, and the welfare of the poor. Entries in the vestry minutes range from the basic: 26th December 1750: a Widow Goose being given a gown, two shifts, and a pair of shoes and stockings; to the large scale: the decisions to open a workhouse and a charity school in 1752 and 1758 respectively.

Law and order were also on the agenda, and in addition to discussions about petty vandalism and theft, a proposal was put forward in 1751 to close the 'Red Lyon Publick House' (in Church Road) for the playing of cards and dice on the Sabbath (see separate entry for Red Lyon). The vestry meetings were attended by anyone liable to pay the poor rate, and even on one occasion by the Prime Minister himself – William Pitt. St. Mary's was in need of a new steeple and at the vestry meeting of May 17th 1787 Pitt offered £125 for a new one.

By 1780 there was a regular stagecoach service three times a week to London via Putney from the Rose & Crown. The 'Wimbledon Machine' not only carried passengers but also brought the London newspapers to Wimbledon, and in the next century was doubling as a postal service.

As noted above, the inn was also a meeting place for the local friendly society. These groups were made up of Villagers who contributed to a fund to be drawn on when any of its members were sick or unemployed.

The Wimbledon Friendly Society, formed in 1745, was one of the earliest, and required of its members a joining fee of 5d and a monthly subscription of 3d. If a member was sick they were entitled to 7d a week. In the event of a member's death £3 was allocated for funeral expenses, £4 went to the next of kin, and ten shillings to the vicar for conducting the service. All the other members were obliged to attend the funeral, and were liable to a fine if they didn't. This obligation was waived however, if the member had died of the 'French pox'. The Friendly Society is believed to have lasted until around 1860.

Earlier that century the Rose & Crown had become a favourite haunt of the poet Leigh Hunt, and later of Algernon Swinburne. Hunt came to Wimbledon on the advice of his doctor who had recommended the fresh air for his 'cough of some years growth'. Hunt lived almost opposite the Rose & Crown and invited literary friends such as John Forster, Bryan Procter and W.M. Thackeray to the inn. Here they would play bagatelle, eat dinner, and stroll on the common. Thackeray described the common as 'noble', and the air and the green country as 'delightfully fresh'. Hunt too loved the common, speaking of its 'Cloth of gold covering of furze'.

Swinburne lived at no.2 the Pines in Putney from 1879 until his death in 1909, and walked daily across the common to his 'local', the Rose & Crown. He avoided the company of other drinkers though, and if approached would escape to a private room. On one occasion, someone is reputed to have attempted to sketch the poet at the inn, at which he departed hurriedly from a side exit. Perhaps one of the earliest instances of harassment by the paparazzi!

Swinburne's chair was until recently still kept upstairs at the pub, and may have been removed from the bar due to the complaints of one landlady in the 1960s who had tourists asking her to pose for photographs in the chair seated on their laps.

In 1954 there was drama at the Rose & Crown when on July 5th two men broke into the pub and blew open the safe. It must have been a very good night at the pub the evening before as none of the occupants heard the explosion. Luckily, it *was* heard by a policeman three hundred yards away! The two men were duly caught and jailed and the court recorder commented drily that pub's occupants 'must sleep very soundly'.

In modern times the Rose & Crown continues much as before – a traditional English inn free of modern gimmicks serving good beer in a congenial atmosphere. It has been owned by Young's since 1860, and in 1970 won the Evening Standard Pub of the Year award.

SWAN

The first reference to a pub on this site is in a directory of 1855 when the owner was Matthew Matthews, and it may well have started as a simple beer shop. By 1860 it is being referred to as the Swan, or the New Swan Inn – perhaps to distinguish it from the original Swan in Church Road which closed down in the 1820s. So it was now the second pub on the Ridgway which was now growing as a small separate community south of the village.

Photographs of the Swan earlier this century show the entrance framed between two large stone pillars, and these are said to have come from Cottenham Park House - the country seat of the second Duke of Wellington. It was the first Duke of Wellington ironically who had introduced the notorious 1830 Beer Act which led to the proliferation of pubs in Wimbledon and elsewhere.

The Cottenham Park Estate was demolished in 1863, and the grand entrance porch it bequeathed to the Swan was itself destroyed a century later in 1969 when a lorry crashed into it.

There had been a livery stable at the side of the Swan since at least 1867, at which time Matthew Matthews is listed as both 'beer retailer' and 'livery stable keeper'. Although the Swan was too late for the coaching age, horse-drawn carriages could be hired from here to the station, which had opened in 1838, bringing in a new era of transport to Wimbledon. The stables survive to this day and are now used as a riding school.

In recent times there have been reports of ghostly activity at the pub and Sian Horn, the manageress in 1994, recounted several problems she and her staff had experienced there. A glass was seen moving across a level table seemingly unaided and the jukebox would turn itself on during the night. On one occasion several members of staff witnessed a glass of beer exploding as someone lifted it, sending glass everywhere, but leaving the beer momentarily suspended in the air before flooding the table.* Thankfully, the ghostly goings on seem to have abated since last experienced in August 1994.

The Swan is now owned by Scottish & Newcastle and has recently been refurbished in traditional pub style, with polished floorboards, wooden barrels, etc. It has a small beer garden at the front which overlooks the house at the corner of Lauriston Road where Poet Laureate Robert Graves was born in 1895.

*A fuller description of the haunting can be found in *Mysterious Wimbledon* by this author and Ruth Murphy.

The Ridgway, Wimbledon.

SWAN c.1910

BALDFACED STAG

Although this was not a Wimbledon Village inn it is the one exception which begs to be included because of its position at the edge of the Common, its importance to the Villagers, and not least because of its colourful history. Any pub which has been the hideout for a gang of highwaymen, a stopping point for Queen Victoria, and a workshop for a famous racing driver simply has to be included.

Now long gone, the inn stood at the junction of present day Stag Lane and Roehampton Vale, a once remote spot along the old Portsmouth Road. The inn had become established by 1663, and may have been here as early as 1650 when the land was first leased out by Dorothy Cecil, co-heir of Edward Viscount Wimbledon.

The original name of the inn was the White Hart, often known as the Halfway House due to its position roughly halfway between Wandsworth and Kingston. It was on the main coaching route between London and Portsmouth on the lands known as Misselden and Newlands – where Newlands farm was later established. It is said that Queen Victoria would later stop at the inn for the first change of horses on her trips from London to Windsor.

It is not known exactly when the inn changed its name to the Baldfaced Stag but this name was used on the map drawn by John Coris in 1787. It was soon after this that it became the headquarters for a local band of highwaymen led by Jerry Abershaw. He and his men worked this area between 1790 when Abershaw was just seventeen years old and 1795 when he was eventually hanged at Kennington Common for shooting dead a Bow Street Runner. His body was brought back to Wimbledon and hung in chains near the Baldfaced Stag on what is now known as Jerry's Hill.*

The remote location of the inn lent itself not only to the misdeeds of highwaymen but to other clandestine activities too. In the late 18th century the area near Jerry's Hill was a favourite spot for bare-knuckle prize-fights, and being the nearest inn the Baldfaced Stag was very probably the most suitable venue for some of the crowd to meet and set wagers.

One of the best-remembered prize-fights fought here was on the 24th of January 1804 between Edward Burke and Henry 'Game Chicken' Pearse. The purse was £100 (a huge sum at the time, roughly four years wages for an agricultural labourer) with £90 to the winner and £10 to the loser. The fight went on for a gruelling twenty-eight rounds and lasted well over an hour.

Many duels were also fought at the same spot or nearby, and the Baldfaced Stag would have been the most convenient place for an after-duel tipple, which was no doubt much needed. It has been said that duellists would sometimes go to an inn prior to their confrontation and ominously order 'pistols for two and breakfast for one'.**

---

* Further details regarding the exploits of Jerry Abershaw can be found in *Mysterious Wimbledon* and *More Mysterious Wimbledon* by this author and Ruth Murphy.

** Further details of duelling on the Common can be found in *Mysterious Wimbledon.*

BALDFACED STAG (THE TALLEST BUILDING) 1881
WITH NEWLANDS FARM TO RIGHT

The landlord of the inn appears in local records in 1807 when he is accused of 'hawking and selling beer and other liquors to the great detriment of Wimbledon innkeepers.' The small community of Wimbledon already had three inns and taverns at this time and they clearly needed no additional competition.

The Baldfaced Stag continued as an inn until at least 1867 but had become a private house by the 1880s. A woman of 82 quoted in the Wimbledon Borough News in 1954 remembers moving to the house as a child in 1881 and even finding Abershaw's gibbet at Jerry's Hill 'steadily mouldering away but still with a chain hanging from it.'

The building survived into the 20th century and by 1912 was being used by racing car driver Kenelm Lee Guinness. It was here that he built his Sunbeam car and went on to set the land speed record with it in 1922, achieving 133 mph at Brooklands. The car was later bought and adapted by Malcolm Campbell, renamed Bluebird and used to set a new land speed record in 1924 at Pendine Sands in Wales.

Kenelm Lee Guinness meanwhile was using the old Baldfaced Stag building as a factory for making spark plugs and by 1918 the KLG factory employed 1200 workers and was the largest employer in the Putney and Roehampton area. The building was finally demolished in 1937 when Smiths Industries, who had taken over the business, built a new factory there. A sad and prosaic end to what had been one of the Common's most colourful inns.

BEWARE THE HIGHWAYMAN!
Scores of pubs up and down the country claim associations with Dick Turpin, but if he had drunk in all of them he probably would have been unable to stand, let alone deliver his famous ultimatum. The only well-documented local highwayman is Jerry Abershaw.

BEEHIVE

The Beehive is one of Wimbledon's best-kept secrets. Aside from one or two oblique mentions nothing much seems to be known about it apart from an article in the Wimbledon Borough News in the 1920s.

In the mid-19th century, just north of the Dog & Fox inn in the High Street were Mutton Row and Dog & Fox Court (now Allington Close). This locality was known as Beehive Place, a collection of slums which were eventually demolished in 1869 to make way for 'improved workmen's dwellings' instigated by the then Earl Spencer.

The 'Beehive' slums were inhabited by large families headed by agricultural labourers, charwomen, gardeners, etc. plus in 1838 by one John Harris, beer retailer, who by 1841 was also listed as a brewer. He was running the Beehive pub, which was described by the Wimbledon Borough News as follows:

'The Landlord is remembered over and above for having provided a splendid blackboard for the children to make lightning sketches upon as they dashed away to the Rounds School* beyond the old wide Wimbledon Green before he could catch them at their art. He objected of course to their impromptu decorations because the "blackboard" formed part of the wall of his house. As for himself, his name was Brown**, and he had the reputation of freely sampling his own cellar, thus earning an obvious nickname.

The Beehive stood at the angle of the path along old Mutton Row – a Row that is now lined with blocks which in the sixties were described as "improved workmen's dwellings". The bricks they are built from came out of the Lord of the Manor's own brickfield...it having been brought to the notice of his Lordship that there was a disreputable part of Wimbledon called "Dog & Fox Court" and "Mutton Row" in which were very poor houses, the dwellings of some of the worst characters of the place, and that a permanent benefit to the parish as well as to the poor occupants might be effected by the purchase of the freehold land and cottages by pulling down all the old houses which were of irregular form and varying height from one to three storeys, and building thereon some forty or fifty flats...a virtue was made of a necessity and the forty resulting tenements proved a great boon to this class of tenants. Another boon must have been the removal of "The Beehive"'.

Well! It certainly seemed to be little short of a crime to be poor in those days, and the Beehive could have been opened to serve those people who may not have been welcome in the rather grander Dog & Fox Hotel just round the corner. Surprisingly, the 'Beehive Buildings' (officially known as the Spencer Buildings) remained for almost a century until they were replaced in 1975 by the Haygarth Place development.

The Beehive would almost certainly have been yet another product of the 1830 Beer Act when anyone who could afford two guineas for an excise licence could run a pub. Before that none of these poorly paid workers would have been able to afford it, or be deemed by local JPs to be of sufficiently high moral character to become a landlord.

* The charity school in Camp Road
**Presumably a later landlord than John Harris

COCK & HOOPE

The Cock & Hoope is one of the most obscure of all Wimbledon Village's long-lost pubs. The only reference to it is in the vestry minutes of 1747; the entry for May 10th reading: 'It was agreed at the bench of justices held April 27th 1747 that the Cock & Hoope house be charged according to the rent paid.' It is likely that the Cock & Hoope was a simple ale house, and probably a short-lived one at that as there is no other mention of it in any of the surveys or maps from that period. All it leaves to us is its unusual name (see Names section).

SAGE ADVICE

Hermit hoar in solemn cell wearing out life's evening gray
Strike thy bosom sage! And tell what is bliss and which the way?
Thus I spoke, and speaking sighed, scarce repressed the starting tear
When the hoary sage replied 'Come my lad and drink some beer'

Dr. Samuel Johnson

JOLLY BUTCHERS

The Jolly Butchers still stands in Church Road but you wouldn't know it as it has now been incorporated into the Castle. The division can clearly be seen at the roof level where above the façade there are two distinctly separate buildings. The Jolly Butchers stood at no.15 Church Road, and the Castle to the east of it at no.16, though the road numbering has of course since changed.

Built later than the late-Georgian Castle, the Jolly Butchers first appears in the records as late as 1874 when it was being run by George Cousens who is described as 'beer retailer and shopkeeper'. Perhaps like William Holland at the Hand in Hand he had started selling beer as a sideline to his main business. By 1878 the 'Butchers' had been taken over by Caroline Cousens, presumably George's widow.

Despite the fact that the 'Butchers' was a simple Victorian beer shop, Henry Cullimore, landlord at the Castle may not have been too pleased with this competition literally on his doorstep. However, one source states that the Castle served the local gentry while the lowlier Jolly Butchers catered for their servants. The pub was even said to have had sawdust on the floor – very appropriate considering its name.

The two pubs existed separately until 1902, but when they merged the following year the new pub was known as the Jolly Butchers for a couple of years until 1905 when for some reason the name reverted to The Castle. The Castle had been bought by the brewery Thorne Brothers in 1900 and the 'Butchers' must have been acquired at around the same time from owners Mann & Crossman of the Albion Brewery in Mile End Road. So although the last pub to appear in Wimbledon Village, the Jolly Butchers was one of the first to go - even though it lives on as half of the Castle.

JOLLY GARDENERS

In the early 19th century the Ridgway was just a country lane. There was nothing along the north side apart from the back gardens of the large houses on the Common, and nothing at all on the south side; just fields, and views across London and the South Downs. But now, with the population of the Village growing, more housing was needed – especially for the poor.

Brickfield Cottages, now Oldfield Road, were put up by William Eades around 1815, and then in the early 1820s local builder William Croft erected more property around present day Denmark Road and Thornton Hill. This consisted of twenty-nine cottages and a beer house named the Jolly Gardeners which was the predecessor to the King of Denmark.

There is no record of who ran the pub when it was first built, but by 1838 the beer retailer listed in the local rate book is Thomas Underwood, and the Jolly Gardeners is owned by William Croft.

It is possible that Mr Croft's son Thomas was the first person to run the beer house as he is listed as a beer retailer in the directory of 1832. However, as his father also owned the Union beer shop in Camp Road at this time it is possible that he may have been based there.

So the Jolly Gardeners was the first 'pub' on the Ridgway, and being a simple beer shop was probably only frequented by the poorer inhabitants of the modest little cottages that were now beginning to change the Ridgway from a country lane into an extension of the Village.

As the century progressed more cottages were built, and in the 1860s the parade of shops known as Denmark Terrace was erected. This of course included the King of Denmark pub from which it got its name. It is not known exactly when the Jolly Gardeners was closed, but it now clearly had a successor, and another Victorian beer shop became a part of Wimbledon Village history.

A DESCRIPTION OF WIMBLEDON IN 1824

A small village, delightfully situated in the county of Surry (sic), distant from the metropolis seven miles. It has an antique church on the entrance of the village. Holds a pleasure fair on the first Monday after Lady Day. The seats of Lords Spencer and Melville are at this place; that of Lord Spencer has a fine and extensive park. Wimbledon appears to have some great attractions, as 'tis the preferred residence of many of our representatives and nobility. The curacy of Wimbledon is perpetual and the Lord of the Manor is Lord Spencer. The population is 2,195.

LORD PALMERSTON

It had been thought up to now that the Lord Palmerston was the predecessor to the Brewery Tap but local directories show that it was a separate beer house in its own right. It existed several doors away up the High Street north of the Brewery Tap at the corner of Lancaster Gardens.

There is very little information available about the pub but the first reference to the landlord James Brown was in 1855 – a date which may also explain the origin of the pub's name (see Names section).

James Brown disappears from the records in 1868, but in 1870, for that year only a Thomas Brown is listed as a beer retailer in the High Street. His beer house unfortunately is not named but he may well have been a son who carried on his father's business after his retirement or death.

It is probably unsurprising that there is little information about the Lord Palmerston as it was just another Victorian beer house with nothing to distinguish it from all the others which had sprung up in the wake of the 1830 Beer Act. This proliferation of beer shops as well as the number of long-established inns and taverns meant of course that competition was fierce and perhaps the Lord Palmerston did well to survive for as long as fifteen years.

Ironically, the business which took over the site of the Lord Palmerston in 1884 was the Welcome Coffee Rooms which had moved from its original, smaller site in Church Road. Coffee rooms such as these were encouraged by the local temperance supporters to entice men away from the pubs so they may have seen this as some measure of success.

THE WATNEY WINDMILL
If John Watney had had his way there would now be a very different windmill on the Common. In 1799 Watney, an ancestor of the famous brewing family, applied to the manor court to build a windmill on the common but he did not submit detailed plans and the proposal was shelved. Watney died in 1814, and by 1817 the construction of the present windmill had begun.

LYON

For the scant information available on the Lyon we are indebted to the 17th century 'Water Poet' John Taylor. A traveller, wanderer and alehouse aficionado, the poet had made it his business to visit inns, taverns, and alehouses and report on them.

In 1637 he published his Carriers' Cosmographie which detailed the labyrinth communications network of carrier services, prior to the stagecoach era, between inns in London and the Home Counties.

His travels took him to all parts of the country and his reports, which predate the diaries of Samuel Pepys, provide an invaluable picture of the inns and taverns of the time. His account of the Rose & Crown inn at Nether Stowey in 1649 includes the following: *'Mine host was sufficiently drunk, the house most delicately decked with artificial and natural sluttery... the walls and ceilings were adorned and hanged with rare spiders' tapestry... the odours and contagious perfume of that house was able to outflight all the milliners in Christendom...'*

With inns such as this to contend with it is perhaps surprising that he had undertaken to compile a list, which was published in 1636, of all the taverns within a thirty-mile radius of London – a total of 686. But this he did, and his travels brought him to Wimbledon where he found three taverns, which he listed as: 'The two Lyons and the Wheat-sheafe.' In this book, A Catalogue of Taverns in the Ten Shires About London he gives no further information about these taverns, although we do know a little about the Red Lyon which was in Church Road (see separate entry).

The Lyon may not appear in other local records as it was a simple tavern rather than a more substantial inn. The two Wimbledon inns at this time, The Sign of My Lord's Arms and the White Hart for example had been mentioned twenty years earlier in the survey of 1617.

So, a tantalising glimpse of another of Wimbledon's earliest drinking houses, but judging by John Taylor's scathing description of the Rose & Crown at Nether Stowey it is perhaps just as well that no further details were given.

As for John Taylor, he ended up becoming a landlord himself; first at Oxford, and then at Long Acre in London where he renamed his inn the Poet's Head and hung a sign outside bearing his own portrait! Also on the sign was one of his own rhyming couplets:

> *There's many a head stands for a sign*
> *Then gentle reader, why not mine?*

RED LYON

We have slightly more information on the Red Lyon than that which John Taylor provides due to the fact that the landlord John Eades had fallen foul of the local authorities.

The playing of cards and dice had been banned as early as 1326 by King Edward III, who considered that these games would divert men from more important duties such as archery practice. And in 1710 the specific dice game of Hazard, an early form of the American game craps, was declared illegal.

So when the local vestry committee learned in 1751 that the Red Lyon in Church Road had been the venue for dice and card games – *and* played on the Sabbath no less - they agreed to have the tavern closed down.

But could this have simply been an excuse rather than a reason to suppress the Red Lyon? Although the playing of cards and dice was officially illegal the law was widely flouted, and the banned games were said to be played not only by the middle and upper classes but by royalty too!

Could it have simply been that the Red Lyon was one drinking house too many in a village of five hundred people which had no fewer than five other such establishments? (The Dog & Fox, The Rose & Crown, The Crooked Billet, The Rising Sun, and The Swan – also in Church Road)

And who were the leading members of the vestry committee who recommended the closure? Why, none other than Edward Winchester, Richard Carter, Thomas Wray, Joseph Freeman, and Joseph Townsend – the landlords of the above inns and taverns!

The original order from the bench of justices had been to 'reduce the number of publick houses in the parish', but the decision on which one was to go was made by the vestry committee. It seems odd that a mere six months earlier, on May 5th, The Red Lyon had been deemed sufficiently respectable to be the venue for a vestry meeting but was now only fit for closure.

So the Red Lyon, which had been there since at least the 1630s when visited by the poet John Taylor, finally closed its doors in 1755 when its licence renewal was turned down leaving the Villagers with a mere five drinking venues from which to choose. (The Red Lyon stood to the east of the earlier White Hart/Swan, which was roughly opposite the present-day Castle).

But if at the church they would give us some ale
And a pleasant fire our souls to regale
We'd sing and we'd pray all the livelong day
Nor ever once wish from the Church to stray

William Blake

RISING SUN

How many people have walked past this house on the common not realising that it is another of Wimbledon Village's long-lost pubs?

It was closed down in 1785 when the local authorities declared it 'injurious to the good order of society', and its licence renewal was refused in 1798.

The Rising Sun first appears in the records in 1745 when Joseph Townsend was landlord and it was being used as a meeting place for the local vestry committee. It is described on the 1776 map of the manor as an alehouse, but its size and commanding position overlooking the common hint that it was a substantial one, unlike the tiny back-street beer houses which appeared in the next century.

What may have sealed the fate of this alehouse was the fact that it was a favourite with the inhabitants of the workhouse round the corner in Camp Road (then Workhouse Lane).

The workhouse, just to the west of where the Fox & Grapes now stands, was built in 1752 on the initiative of the vestry committee. Its rules banned the drinking of gin amongst other things, but it is interesting to note that in the workhouse accounts of 1775 a pint and a half of gin had been purchased at a cost of 3d (the same price then as a loaf of bread!)

The Rising Sun undoubtedly provided a change of scene, some form of entertainment, and a more convivial atmosphere than that of the workhouse; plus of course, relatively cheap ale ('small beer' was only a penny halfpenny a gallon in the middle of the 18th century).

By the 1760s Westside had an impressive line of large houses and the Rising Sun must have been something of a thorn amongst these roses. It was flanked by Cannizaro House (then Warren House) to the south, and Stamford House to the north, with Westside House and Chester House nearby; the latter said to have been built for a mistress of James II.

In 1798, thirteen years after the Rising Sun had been closed down the vestry committee received a letter signed by forty-two of the poorer residents of Westside asking for the renewal of the alehouse's licence. They complained of the inconvenience of having to fetch their beer from the Rose & Crown or Dog & Fox in the Village (the nearby Crooked Billet too had closed by this time). The application was forwarded to the local magistrates at Putney but the request was refused.

The house, which still stands today, is now divided into two dwellings, but in one of them the name of the Rising Sun lives on.

SWAN (CHURCH ROAD)

The Swan was successor to the White Hart in Church Road which itself had been in existence since perhaps the 1540s (see separate entry). The new name first appears in 1757 when the Swan, which was being run by Joseph Freeman, was yet another meeting place for the vestry committee. It was after all, the inn nearest to St. Mary's Church. There had been references to vestry meetings at Joseph Freeman's as early as 1748 but the name of the inn was not specified.

It had been thought that the Swan had closed around 1785, but the list of Surrey Victuallers (which unfortunately only goes up to 1804) is still showing the Swan being run as late as 1804 by Joseph Woodman. However, by the time the Victuallers Recognizance list was published in 1825 the Swan is no longer mentioned. Ironically, there is more information available on the Swan's predecessor, the White Hart (see separate entry).

UNION BEER HOUSE

The predecessor to the Fox & Grapes in Camp Road, and first mentioned as the Union beer house in 1838 when run by Charles Taylor. There is then a gap in the records when it may have been closed. The next landlord is one William Fisher, listed in 1845 and 1846 only. There is then another gap in the records until 1860 when William Mayes is listed in local directories as 'beer retailer and carpenter'. The following year he has been replaced by John Cordery whose family ran the pub for the next twenty years. By now it had become the Fox & Grapes (see separate entry).

WHEAT-SHEAFE

The third of the three Wimbledon taverns listed in John Taylor's survey of 1636 (see entry for Lyon), but unfortunately no other mention is recorded elsewhere.

WHITE HART

Listed in Treswell's survey of 1617 the White Hart may well have existed as early as the 1540s when a Gyles Smith was mentioned several times in the manor court rolls for various misdemeanours. He was known as 'a tavern keeper of Church Way' (now Church Road) – although the name of the tavern at this time is not listed. He was in trouble for, amongst other things, selling his beer at too high a price.

In 1585 the Village constable Giles Cole had the job of collecting taxes from all the inhabitants of Wimbledon, a mere 44 households, and fortunately this list survives. From this we find that the landlord of the White Hart is now Henry Savage who had bought the house from Gyles Smith's son Thomas.

In 1617, when the survey of the manor was commissioned by Thomas Cecil, the White Hart was described as consisting of 'five rooms, a barn, a shed, and an orchard.' It was one of only two drinking establishments in the village at the time – the other being the Sign Of My Lord's Arms, the predecessor to the Dog & Fox. It is likely that the White Hart was a tavern, catering for locals rather than an inn as unlike the Sign Of My Lord's Arms it had no stabling for travellers.

It is not known exactly when the White Hart ceased to exist under that name but by the 1740s it had been renamed the Swan (see separate entry)

THE EVILS OF DRINK

The fourth immorality which our laws endeavour to suppress is drunkenness: a vice on which one of our statutes fixes this infamous character; that it is odious and loathsom, that it is the root and foundation of bloodshed, stabbing, murther, swearing, fornication, adultery and such like enormous sins, to the dishonour of God and of our nation, the overthrow of many good arts, and manual trades, the disabling of divers workmen, and the general impoverishment of many good subjects abusively wasting the good creatures of God.

Decree by Surrey Magistrates 5th of April 1692

THE PUB NAMES

Behind many a pub name lies a story, and the pubs of Wimbledon Village are no exception. In this section are the backgrounds to the names of all the pubs, past and present, mentioned in this booklet. In fact, some of the pub names go back to a time before the idea of naming pubs was even thought of. That sounds like a contradiction, but the pub names came from their signs, which were hung outside taverns and inns for the many prospective customers who were illiterate.

So for example, an alehouse keeper may have hung a misshapen log (sometimes known as a billet) outside his house to mark it out from other mere dwelling houses, and it would become known as The Sign of the Crooked Billet. Later on, a sign showing a crooked billet would have been hung outside instead, and so the inn sign was born. From the time of Richard II it was compulsory for publicans to show a sign outside their house, even though it may have been of the hanging log variety.

The other reason that a sign of some sort was necessary was because the official inspector, or ale connor, of medieval times needed to be able to find at which houses he had to sample the ale.

Of course, in later centuries the inn sign started to become almost an art form in itself, and the names began to become more outlandish. Though it is only in recent years that pub names have become pure inventions rather than relating to some historical person or event, or local tradition.

The traditional pub name can usually tell you something interesting about the area, or about history. But a modern pub name of the Rat and Drainpipe variety tells you nothing more than that the head of the brewery's marketing department had probably over-lunched himself on the day he dreamt it up.

One local example is the Brewery Tap. 'Reliable' sources maintain that there has never been a brewery on the site of this pub in Wimbledon Village. But why then does it have this name? After some research it was revealed that there *had* been a brewery there, and that the Brewery Tap pub was almost literally what it sounds to be – the outlet for the brewery's beer (see entry for Brewery Tap).

It would be hoped that breweries could keep up the tradition of naming their pubs appropriately, and not interfere with historic names, but for now let's look at the stories behind the Wimbledon Village pubs.

BALDFACED STAG

Probably a hunting reference. This type of stag, so called owing to the white stripe on its forehead, may well have been hunted locally in the surrounding woodland at the time this inn was built in the 17th century. Stag hunting was certainly going on near Merton Hall Farm as late as the 1880s.

BEEHIVE

The Beehive is not an uncommon name for a pub and is believed to derive from the fact that honey was once used to sweeten ale. However, in this case, it is easy to imagine it starting as a nickname for this back-street beer house, swarming with the inhabitants of the surrounding slums.

BREWERY TAP

As shown earlier, the name comes directly from the associated brewery, which was there by 1832, albeit most probably on a small scale. Though a larger brewery was built in 1885 only to burn down in 1889. The pub, of course, survives.

CASTLE

Another common pub name. At least, common when in close proximity to a castle or the site of one, but was there ever a castle in Wimbledon? Not that can be found, but, the first lessee of the property in Church Road in 1828, before it became a pub, was one William Castle. A wry joke then perhaps by the first publican James Johnson in 1845.

COCK & HOOPE

Fitting perhaps that one of the most obscure pubs in historic Wimbledon should have an equally misleading name. The cock referred to is not the bird of medieval fighting fame, but the tap used to draw beer from the barrel. The hoop is of course that at the top of the barrel, and once the cock was drawn and placed on top of the barrel with the beer freely flowing the customers were said to be cock-a-hoop.

CROOKED BILLET

An ancient pub name and sign as mentioned earlier, but one alternative explanation has been offered. Billet was also another word for staff, and crooked can also be pronounced as one syllable instead of two, so a crooked billet could be something akin to a shepherd's crook. The Common was of course a local grazing place so this explanation cannot be ruled out.

DOG & FOX

The obvious derivation of this name would be from fox-hunting, but there is no record of organised fox-hunting in the area. Though it is known that John, first Spencer Lord of the Manor, was a keen huntsman, being master of the Pytchley Hunt at Althorp.

The previous name of this inn was The Sign of My Lord's Arms (see separate entry), so keeping in with the Lord of the Manor was certainly a tradition that it would have been wise for an ambitious innkeeper to continue! (Between the above two mentioned names, the inn was briefly known as the Fox & Dog, though there is no record of the reason for the change).

FOX & GRAPES

Although there is no local reason for this pub name it comes of course from one of the most famous of Aesop's fables. The fox, unable to reach the grapes at the top of the vine, attempts indifference and asserts that they were probably sour anyway - the original case of sour grapes. Incidentally, the sign currently outside the Village pub isn't quite accurate as it shows the fox reaching the grapes!

HAND IN HAND

There are various explanations for pubs with this name ranging from meeting places for early friendly societies, to the pubs being secular venues for wedding ceremonies. Neither seems to have been the case with this Village pub, but it could simply be that with its close proximity to the Crooked Billet the two pubs could be said to be hand in hand with one another.

JOLLY BUTCHERS

With the proliferation of beer houses in the Victorian era, many of them aimed unashamedly at the working class drinker, whilst the more ornate 'gin palaces' and inns served the lower middle classes. A name such as this would therefore attract the working men whilst their superiors would drink in the classier surroundings of pubs such as the Castle – literally next door.

JOLLY GARDENERS

As above, this appealed directly to the working man, and with the large number of estates and gardens to attend to in the area there can have been no shortage of potential customers.

KING OF DENMARK

There are many Kings of Denmark after whom this pub may have been named, but two in particular are strong candidates. Christian IV came to England in 1606 to visit his brother-in-law James I and the two of them were said to have gone on a three-day drunken binge which was remembered for many years to come. Whether it was in the minds of those who built the pub two hundred and sixty years later though is another matter.

Perhaps a more likely explanation is that there was an upsurge of royal feeling when Edward VII married Princess Alexandra, daughter of the King of Denmark in 1863, just before the pub was built. This may also explain the naming of the Alexandra pub in Wimbledon.

LORD PALMERSTON

This pub started as a beer house in 1855, the year that Henry John Temple (Lord Palmerston) first became Prime Minister. The association with a man who was to become a popular Prime Minister can have done the pub no harm with the drinking public.

LYON

Merely an alternative spelling of lion which is an ancient heraldic symbol indicating strength. Many early pub signs were based on heraldic symbols, being easily recognisable to the people they wished to attract, many of whom were illiterate.

RED LYON

Red Lion is the commonest pub name in England, and derives from the symbol of John of Gaunt, the 14th century nobleman who effectively ruled England during the last years of the reign of Edward III who was by then senile.

ROSE & CROWN

The Wimbledon Village pub was originally known as The Sign of the Rose. It was built in the 1650s during the period between the reigns of Charles I and Charles II when Oliver Cromwell was Lord Protector. Keeping in line with public feeling was obviously important for an innkeeper, and the 'Crown' was later added to the name as it was to the head of Charles II. The rose of course was and is a national symbol for England.

SIGN OF MY LORD'S ARMS

The lord in question was of course the first lord of the manor of Wimbledon, Thomas Cecil, the Earl of Exeter. So the sign which hung outside the inn would have been the two rampant lions from the Cecil coat of arms. It was common at one time for inns to show the arms of nobility associated with their area, hence the numerous pubs with 'arms' in their name, and naturally, to honour his lord in such a way would have done no harm to the innkeeper's relationship with him.

THE CECIL COAT OF ARMS

SUN (ALSO KNOWN AS RISING SUN)

Another heraldic symbol, often associated with Edward III, i.e. the sun of York. However, a simpler explanation may be that the pub was eastwards facing.

SWAN

Often featured in royal coats of arms such as those of Henry V and Henry VIII. Again, a simple, easily recognisable sign. The swan was also a symbol connected with vintners' companies. A recent inn sign outside the present day Swan in Ridgway was meant to depict a Swan alighting on the Queensmere pond at Wimbledon Common.

UNION

There was a beer house here by 1832, and the 'union' probably refers to the Act of Union between Great Britain and Ireland in 1801. Of course this union was foundering later in that century – perhaps it was this that led to the change of name to The Fox & Grapes. Could it be that this choice of name indicated Britain's new attitude to Ireland, and like the fox with the grapes we claimed not to have really wanted it/them in the first place?

WHEAT-SHEAFE

One of the earliest signs, which was made with an actual sheaf of wheat, and was once a symbol denoting a bakery. It was often used by houses that brewed beer as well as baked bread. A relatively recent example of this type of house is the Hand in Hand pub at Wimbledon Common, which started in the nineteenth century as a bakehouse and later sold beer.

WHITE HART

Originally the badge of Richard II, this remained a very popular pub name long after its initial association had been forgotten, and was again, a simple distinctive sign chosen mainly for its visual immediacy.

In Putney High Street in the 18th century was an inn of some importance to the inhabitants of Wimbledon. The White Lion was the convening place for the local magistrates. It was here for example that the decision was made to close the Rising Sun at Wimbledon Common. Sadly, the memory of a once-important inn was destroyed when it was recently renamed the Slug & Lettuce.
Another example of this was when the White Hart in Kingston Road, Wimbledon was recently renamed Bodhran Barney's. Under its old name it had not only been the venue for the manor court but also for the sale of Lord Nelson's Estate on September 16th 1823.

BREWING IN WIMBLEDON

As nothing remains of it today it may surprise some people to find that there was once a tradition of brewing in Wimbledon. In fact one of the most famous names of the brewing business can be found here in the 1700s.

Although the famous brewery empire was not begun until a couple of generations later, William Watney ran the Wheatsheaf Brewery in the Crooked Billet area in the 18th century. William's father Daniel had moved to Wimbledon in the 1730s, and lived in a cottage on the site of the present day Hand in Hand. One of Daniel's other sons, John, prospered and built Rushmere House, which still stands today as part of the King's College School just opposite the Crooked Billet. Even Daniel's daughter Mary played a part in the pub history of Wimbledon by marrying Samuel Mason, the landlord of the Rose & Crown.

The Spencer map of 1776 shows William's Wheatsheaf brewery next to his cottage just to the west of where the Crooked Billet pub stands today. The same map also shows a Dr. Gears Esq. who has a 'brewhouse' along Southside. With his title it is unlikely that he was a competitor of Watney's but probably brewed beer for himself.

The Wheatsheaf Brewery continued after the death of William Watney and by 1824 was being run by Isaac Hellier. His son George took over around 1845 but by 1846 the brewery disappears from the records.

Perhaps it was feeling the competition from the Wimbledon Brewery in the High Street. This had been started by William Cook by 1832 and stood at the site of where the old fire station building stands opposite the Dog & Fox today. Next door to it, to the north was the Brewery Tap beer house, also run by William Cook.

The Wimbledon Brewery flourished under various owners for most of the rest of the century, and in 1885 was rebuilt by William Quartermaine who had taken over five years previously. The new brewery was five stories high and the tallest building in Wimbledon. Unfortunately it burned down in 1889 (see next page).

Shortly after this, in 1891, there was a Swan Brewery depot next to the site at no. 1 Church Road, although the brewery itself was in Fulham. Also, around the same time the Anglo-Bavarian Brewery is listed as being at 36 Wimbledon Hill Road, and it remained there until 1909.

Perhaps the most exclusive 'brewery' ever in Wimbledon was that of William Cecil, Lord of the Manor who moved into the rectory at St. Mary's church in 1550. A personal brewhouse was probably essential for a large household in those days and the nearest and only inn in Wimbledon Village at that time was that at the Sign of My Lord's Arms.

Today of course, the nearest independent brewery is Young & Co. at Wandsworth, and they own four, arguably four of the most historic of the existing Wimbledon Village pubs – the Rose & Crown, Dog & Fox, Crooked Billet, and Hand in Hand.

THE WIMBLEDON BREWERY FIRE

This brewery, once next to where the Brewery Tap now stands in the High Street suffered a tragic demise near the end of the last century and the story was reported in the Surrey Independent. In the early hours of Wednesday morning on January 2nd 1889 a fire started at the brewery, but what ensued was a tragi-comedy almost worthy of the Keystone Cops.

Wimbledon Brewery 1889

First on the scene, at 3.15 a.m. was one P.C. Carver who promptly blew his whistle. Unfortunately the men at the nearest fire station in Wimbledon Broadway would have been unable to hear this and P.C. Carver commandeered a passing employee of Standen's Bakery who was dispatched to alert the fire brigade. The baker's boy however was not fleet of foot and didn't arrive there until some 35 minutes later.

Once alerted, the firemen fetched and harnessed the horses and started their journey to the now raging fire. It being an icy night, they decided to avoid the treacherous Wimbledon Hill and elected instead to go via St Mary's Road. The wily ice however, had found its way there also, and the firemen struggled to get the engine to the top, having at times, to get out and push the thing. Eventually they arrived at the scene, it now being more than an hour since the blaze had first been discovered.

Unfortunately, there was now another delay: the engine fire which powered the pumps was low, and before fire fighting could commence it needed more fuel. Someone was sent to find wood. Once the steam engine was roaring again the fire fighting began. The blaze, having now 'obtained a great mastery' as the Surrey Independent put it, was difficult to control, but around 6.00 a.m. the firemen suddenly had some luck. The water tank on the top floor of the brewery crashed through the entire five-storey building and in a matter of seconds did more to douse the flames than the firemen had achieved in all of the preceding one hundred and twenty minutes.

The inferno now at last under control, the brigade decided to unhitch the engine and fix a stand-pipe just across the road (opposite the old Welcome Cafe). There was only one problem: the fire-plug had inexplicably been buried under a heap of granite stones! After much puffing and panting, the stones were cleared only to reveal yet another obstacle: the hosepipe did not fit the fire-plug.

This was overcome by using the pipe from the fire engine, and at long last the blaze was over by 7.00 a.m. By this time of course, every bit of machinery and assorted brewing apparatus had been destroyed, and although it was believed at the time that the brewery could be rebuilt, it never was. It was replaced by – a fire station. What better memorial to this disaster than the Village's first proper fire station (an old fire engine had been kept next to the Fox & Grapes in Camp Road earlier that century, but had probably gone by this time).

ACKNOWLEDGEMENTS

Ruth Murphy
Merton Local Studies Library
Richard Milward
Wimbledon Society
Charles Toase
Surrey Record Office
Julie Jarrott (Allied Domecq)
Ken Thomas (Courage)
Nick Redman (Whitbread)
Clair O' Neill (Scottish Newcastle)
Helen Osborn (Young & Co.)
Anne-Marie Hill (Wimbledon Society)
Simon Bretherton
Ian Dickson
Kevin Jones
John Spain
Brian Ceney
Nigel Headley
Lindsay Klatt

PHOTOGRAPHS/PICTURES

Brewery Tap – Nick Redman (Whitbread)
Castle – Wimbledon Society
Crooked Billet – Wimbledon Society
Dog & Fox – Wimbledon Society
King Of Denmark – Clive Whichelow
Hand In Hand – Wimbledon Society
Fox & Grapes – Clive Whichelow
Rose & Crown – Wimbledon Society
Swan – Clive Whichelow
Baldfaced Stag – Wandsworth Library Service
Wimbledon Brewery – Surrey Independent

BIBLIOGRAPHY

Historic Wimbledon – Richard Milward
Wimbledon 200 Years Ago – Richard Milward
Tudor Wimbledon – Richard Milward
Portrait Of Wimbledon – Richard Milward
The Life And Sport Of The Inn – Michael Brander
The Inn Explorer's Guide – Frank Bottomley
Pub Names Of Great Britain – Leslie Dunkling & Gordon Wright
Introduction To Inn Signs – Eric R. Delderfield
A New View of Old Wimbledon – Gillian Hawtin
Inn & Around London – Helen Osborn
The Old Inns of England – A.E. Richardson